A M S T E R D A M

Photography and compilation
Herman Scholten

BearsPublishingAlmere

COLOFON

Copyright:
Bears Publishing
P.O. Box 1482
1300 BL Almere

Compilation and photography:
Herman Scholten, Almere

Responsible for other photographs:
Fotodienst KLM: *pages 4/5 (4x)*
Capital Press: *page 5 (1x)*
Aerophoto Schiphol: *pages 8/9, 24/25, 120/121, 123 (2x)*
Museum Amstelkring: *page 13 (4x)*
Beeldbank en Uitgeefprojekten: *pages 14 (1x), 21 (2x), 23 (1x), 31 (1x)*
Anne Frank Stichting: *page 39 (1x)*
Amsterdams Historisch Museum: *pages 42 (1x), 43 (1x), 56/57*
Museum van Loon, Maarten Brinkgreve: *pages 46/47(6x)*
Benelux Press: *pages 49 (1x), 72 (1x) 84/85, 107 (1x), 111 (1x) 116/117, 126/127*
Museum Het Rembrandthuis: *pages 58/59 (4x)*
Rijksmuseum: *page 83 (1x)*
Gassan Diamonds: *pages 108/109*

Text: Frederik Wiedijk, Blokzijl

Lithography: Nederlof Repro, Heemstede

Cover design: Tjasker Design, Schellingwoude

Publication and distribution:
Bears Publishing, Almere
Tel: 036 - 530 0003
Fax: 036 - 530 0630

Printed by:
Kampert Drukwerk B.V.
Griekenweg 7
5342 PX Oss

Translation: All English Translations

ISBN Nummer: 90-5495-915-0

Gassan Diamonds B.V. • *Nieuwe Uilenburgerstraat 173-175* • *1011 LN Amsterdam.*
Tel: 020 - 622 53 33 • *Fax: 020 - 624 60 84* • *Open daily from 9.00 till 17.00*

Amsterdam, a city that is very much alive with a rich history.

Amsterdam can undoubtedly be considered as one of the most important and complete historical city centres in the world. It can also be considered to be the nicest and most cultural centre on our planet. The arts and sciences are very highly regarded in Amsterdam.

The Amsterdam mentality is best described as 'jovial', liberal and hospitable. Although the Dutch government is located in Den Haag, Amsterdam is the capital of the country. The population is very proud of its city. This feeling is very much confirmed, especially over the last few years, by the many institutions and societies that have taken strong interest in preserving the Amsterdam heritage and keeping it clean

The attitude of live and let live is very important here. A great number of languages are spoken in this multi-cultural society. Even the Amsterdammers themselves have a great number of dialects. The people who live in the 'Jordaan' area of Amsterdam (where the Dutch language is spoken in a typical Jordaan broad tongue) say that people from the Kattenburg district speak coarse.

Amsterdam is a very sociable place, the fact that there are nearly 1.300 cafés within the municiple bounders speaks for itself. Eating and drinking can go on for almost twenty-four hours a day. There are also a large number of places to go to such as the theatre, music shows, cabaret and other forms of relaxation.

The museum directors want to avoid the image of stuffiness and do their best to provide regularly changing exhibitions with different themes. The history of the city dates back to at least 1275. It was then that a dam was built in the river Amstel that flowed into the inner sea 'the IJ'. Fishermen made their homes near the dam.

At the end of the 14th century the settlement could already be described as a small harbour village. One century later the city built a wall around it. This was during the 'Eighty years of War' with Spain. In 1612 the City Fathers decided to expand the town. Canal after canal was dug enclosing the old city centre with a network of streets and alleys. Unfortunately the building work in the 19th century was without much style. That is why in 1935 the Berlage-plan was developed. Buildings in the expansion area were given more allure.

Yet the old city centre has always been and still is of special beauty. There is a large variety of monuments.

The city centre contains around 20.000 buildings. One third were built before 1850. The government and the municipality have listed 6.700 of these with a preservation order. Another 160 buildings are considered as of great aesthetic importance to Amsterdam.

A lovely variety of gables can be seen along the canals. The merchant's houses, coach-houses and warehouses are rather narrow and deep and have distinguishing gables.

Step, spout, bell, neck, cornice gables are ornamental to these canal houses. Amsterdam is actually built up of over 90 islands that are separated from each other by around 100 kilometres of canal.

The 'islands' are connected by about 400 stone bridges ('locks'). Amsterdam has always moved with the times, even architecturally. At present a new district is being built where soon 18.000 homes will stand. More than half of these homes will be located along the water. On the same water there will be space for a few hundred houseboats and ships such as the ones that are on the existing canals in the city centre.

In this edition we wish to include the latest architectural enterprises such as the 'New Metropolis' on the Oosterdok near Central Station. To really get to know Amsterdam city centre you can do this best by walking or on the bicycle and take time to enjoy the sights. Sights such as the pictures on the more than 650 stone tablets on houses. The Amsterdam Historical Museum has a collection of 48 stone tablets.

The Rijksmuseum (the largest museum in the Netherlands) too has several of the gable stone pictures in its collection.

The Rijksmuseum was built in 1885 by P.H.J. Cuypers and does not only house a large collection of paintings from the Amsterdam Golden Age (such as the Night Watch by Rembrandt), but also a unique collection of doll's houses shaped like canal houses and a Print Room.

This edition can serve as an introduction for a visit to the capital or can be enjoyed as a souvenir following a great trip. During your either 'paper walk' or real wander round the city, please be reminded of the proverb beneath the Amsterdam Coat of Armour: 'Heroism - Determination - Charity'.

Please enjoy reading this book and looking at the photographs.

Air Traffic Control Tower

When watching the bustling activity at the airport Schiphol as it is today, it is very hard to imagine that on this spot the waves of the Haarlemmermeer (lake) once foamed. Around 1855 the lake was milled dry using many windmills and the pump-engine Cruquius (now a museum). '

Amsterdam Airport' now lies (safely), some 4 metres under North Sea-level.

Departure Hall

Departure Lounge

Many international offices and distribution companies are located around the airport. Schiphol, internationally better known as 'Amsterdam Airport', is ideally situated near to the capital.

Air traffic controllers

Train or road connections to other large cities such as Utrecht,
The Hague and Rotterdam are ideal. Travelling to the rest of Holland using domestic flights is also very easy.

Schiphol Airport's shopping centre

It is no wonder that large international companies are located in or near Amsterdam. Schiphol is the home to the KLM fleet. KLM was the first airline company in the world and has operated for over 75 years.

Whether you have just arrived or are leaving, the atmosphere at Central Station surely gives the feeling of being 'in' Amsterdam.

Arrivals are welcomed and departing visitors are sent off by the many musicians, fire-spitters and tramps that hang around the station.

It is definitely not apparent that the station was built at the end of the 19th century on an artificial island specially created on the IJ for this purpose.

The station blocks the clear view over the harbour. Until the station was built Amsterdammers had enjoyed a picturesque view of the sails, flags and smoke from the odd steamer.

Nonetheless with this solution the architect P.H.J. Cuypers prevented the railway line to be built right through the heart of the city.

The building with its mixture of gothic and Dutch renaissance styles has been criticized, but the intention of welcoming travellers through a majestic entrance into the city of Amsterdam has definitely prevailed.

The Arms of the State has been sculptured in the centre of the front gable with a lion on each side. Underneath this the coat of arms of towns such as Berlin, St. Petersburg and Paris (14 in total) can be seen. All these cities can be reached by the railway-connection.

Details of the front of the station

The old city centre of Amsterdam unfolds like an exotic fan. 'Sickle-shaped rows on a carpet of green velvet', this is how a poet from the last century described his city. 'All that water within the brick walls of the winding canals give her a rare and special beauty' was his opinion.

The current city centre of Amsterdam was built progressively (first the Singel, then the Herengracht, Keizersgracht and the Prinsengracht followed like the an extra layer around the middle).

The architectural harmony of these main canals is very clear. The network comes together with connecting canals, picturesque streets and little alleys and resembles the spokes on a wheel.

It is a perfect example of excellent foresight of the city council of the time of the design. Canals were dug out over several centuries by men using spades, wheelbarrows, blood, sweat and tears. The artery of the network was the river Amstel where a dam was built in 1275.

The dam was located exactly where now the Dam and the Royal Palace are situated. At a later time parts of the river Amstel were filled in. These are now called the Rokin and the Damrak.

Islands were created where long ago the Amstel winded its way towards the old Zuider Sea. Examples of these islands are the ones that support the many warehouses and the Central Station.

Follow our lead of the paper trail through this unique city.

Noord-Zuid Hollands Koffiehuis

The original waiting room was built in an old Dutch style and was knocked down to make way for the metro. It was rebuilt using the original bricks and parts of the building.

The Coffee House on the Stationsplein is not only a place where you can have a cup of coffee, as it also houses the Amsterdam tourist office.

The Schreierstoren (Cryers Tower) was part of a defence cordon in the 15th century. This was where fishermen's wives shed their tears when saying goodbye to their husbands going to sea or cry when they did not return. The Schreiers Tower was a silent witness to their sorrows.

Schreiers Tower

Prins Hendrikkade with St. Nicolas Church

St. Nicolas is the patron saint for seamen and ports. The dome and towers of the church dominate the view across from the Central Station. The church was built at the end of the 19th century in honour of the patron saint of the seamen.

The crown that belonged to emperor Maximillian is located on the high altar and is only part of the extensive interior of the church.

Schreiers Tower

Near the station other means of transportation are visible. The bicycle parking area is representative of a cycling city.

Bicycle parking at Central Station

The statue called 't Kolkje is regarded as one of the most picturesque scenes in old Amsterdam. The St. Nicolaas Church dominates the view from here. Behind the Oudezijdskolk is a bridge that leads us to the Zeedijk. The name Zeedijk is derived from the time that the IJ, previously the Zuider Sea, lead all the way into the heart of Amsterdam.

The Zeedijk is specially known for the large variety of small restaurants, eating houses and nice pubs.

The 'warm neighbourhood' now includes the Zeedijk area behind 't Kolkje. A few very nice-looking houses are situated along the Oudezijds Voorburgwal. This canal is clearly broader that the Oudezijds Achterburgwal which lies just behind the Voorburgwal.

The 'Wallen' are not only known in Amsterdam, but by everyone in the Netherlands. It is a term that refers to the 'oldest profession in the world' which has been practised here for centuries.

Oudezijds Voorburgwal

On the corner of the Oudezijds Voorburgwal and the Oudezijds Armsteeg, on number 14, there is a typical Renaissance monument: 'The Burgt of Leiden'. This monument is also known as 'the Leeuwenburg' (the Lionburg) as it shows a stronghold and two lions heads on the step gable (1605).

Behind this beautiful rustic façade, the activities of the Salvation Army are hidden. They have taken it upon themselves to show concern for human suffering in the area.

Oudezijds Voorburgwal nr. 14

It is not obvious to see, but in fact a spacious Baroque Church is located in the attic of the Oudezijds Voorburgwal number 40. The deception is deliberate because when in 1578 the Reformation took place, catholics were only able to practice their religion in secret. That is why the church is named after its location, Ons' Lieve Heer op Solder Kerk (solder means: attic).

From 1887, when the St. Nicolaas Church was opened and Freedom of Religion had been in force for 12 years, the church in the attic was no longer necessary. There were many clandestine churches, but this attic church is the only one remaining.

The church is stilled used for weddings, services and organ concerts.

In 1888 the previously clandestine church was changed into a museum. Authentic living quarters from the 17th and 18th century can be seen here. Many church art-treasures and the small statue of Pater Brugman who died in 1473 are here too. In memory of Brugman's oratorical art there is the Dutch proverb 'praten als Brugman' (talking like Brugman). It is possible to wander on several floors of this unusual house and smallest museum in Amsterdam. The priest's room and the actual church are open to visitors.

The alter can be made partially invisible. Whenever necessary, it was made to disappear behind panels.

The view from the window on the north side is of the St. Nicolas Church and on the south of the showpiece in the area: the Oude Kerk (Old Church).

The oldest building in Amsterdam is a church built in the 13th and 14th century. As time went on many chapels have been added.
This church was dedicated to St. Nicolas too, but as it is the oldest of all churches it is simple called 'Old Church'.

This beautiful monument has a very distinctive tower with a Hemony carillon.

The Weigh House

When the circle of defence was still intact there was a wall that led from the Schreiers Tower to the gateway of the city: the St. Antoniespoort. Later this became the gate known as 'de Waag' (Weigh House).

Public executions took place on the square in front of the Weigh House. Now the Waag is used as a multifunctional building.

Zuiderkerk

Haarlemmersluis (lock)

The 'Amsterdammertjes' can be found all through the city centre. These short cast iron poles are meant to keep the pavements free from parked cars. The Amsterdam people will regard them as art objects and decorate them in any colour.

The house on Singel number 7 is the narrowest house in Amsterdam. It is not much wider than a solid door. When Amsterdam was being built, the tax-levy was calculated by the width of the front of the house.

Round Lutheran Church

The Koepel (Dome) is located on the Singel and was built as a Lutheran Church by Adriaan Dorsman between 1668 and 1671. Lutheran Churches were not permitted to have a tower. Following a large fire the church was rebuilt to its former glory. Unfortunately another fire broke out in the dome in 1993.

This dome was replaced, but it took several years before the copper roof regained its green colour. Presently the monument is no longer used as a church, but congresses, theatre productions and expositions are held here.

Narrowest House on Singel nr. 7

Damrak

Walking from Central Station to the
Royal Palace on the Dam we walk
along the forever busy Damrak with
its many travel agencies, souvenir
shops and other shops.

Most canal cruise boats are moored
in front of the station or nearby.

Damrak

You can see it on people's faces when they arrive in our
capital for the first time. Near bewilderment at the bustling
activity.

If there is anything going on in Amsterdam it definitely
will be here along the part of the river Amstel that has been
filled in.

On the left side of the Damrak we see the Beursplein
(stock exchange square) with a stock exchange complex
designed by the architect Hendrik Petrus Berlage. When it
was opened in 1903 it was considered a much praised,
modern building.

Damrak

Damrak

The former stock exchange building now facilitates exhibitions. There is a permanent exhibition where you can see how the exchange was built and why it was so special. There is also a museum shop.

Beursplein

Looking down from the tower gives a surprising view over the city.

When building the largest townhall in Europe the architect Jacob van Campen introduced the Classicism style into Holland. In 1808 Louis Napoleon decided that the building should be a palace instead. Actually it has hardly ever been used as such.

The Royal Palace does not have an impressive monumental entrance. It was decided that instead an entrance was needed that would be able to withstand possible rebellions.

Palace Hall

Entering the 30 metre high 'Burg-erzaal' will surely be the highlight of the tour of the Royal Palace. It is a hall where the space, the sculptures and paintings all come together in a unique baroque experience.

The sculptures follow a theme: 'necessity for fair governing' and 'jus-tice'. On one side of the hall you will find the Patroness of Amsterdam with the figures of Strength and Wisdom on either side. On the other side Jus-tice is flanked by Death and Punish-ment.

National Monument on the Dam

Directly opposite to the Royal Palace on the Dam you will find the National Monument which symbolises the resistance against the Nazis during the 1940-1945 war. Each year on the 4th of May the fallen are remembered ceremoniously. Weather permitting, young people from all over the world gather on the steps that lead to the memorial.

The National Monument is a creation of the famous Dutch sculptor, painter, designer and lithographer Johan Anton Raedecker (1885 -1956). He designed it together with the architect J.J.P. Oud.

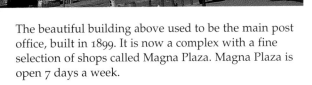

The Bijenkorf

Near the National Monument is the well known department store 'The Bijenkorf'. The photograph on the left shows the interior at Christmas. Amsterdam is known for its selection of fashion-houses.

Shops with antiques and rarities are mainly located around the Rijksmuseum (Spiegelstraat). Their reputation is world wide.

Magna Plaza

The beautiful building above used to be the main post office, built in 1899. It is now a complex with a fine selection of shops called Magna Plaza. Magna Plaza is open 7 days a week.

'Bird's eye view of the Heart of Amsterdam' is the caption for this impressive aerial photograph.

It must be wonderful to be able to fly like a bird above this city. Just like 'the pigeons on the Dam' that are celebrated in songs all over the world. The pigeons that live there have a good life, they are fed every day.

The Palace on the Dam used to be the City Hall. The Palace, with the large Dam square and the Resistance Monument in front of it, is prominently in the foreground.

We glance along the Damrak and the Red Light District to the top right of the picture to the see the new housing estate on the KNSM island.

There is surprising to see that the large amount of green between all that stone and concrete is very much treasured in Amsterdam.

'How much joy (and sorrow) will there be shared under the many different roofs'. That is what our pigeon could ask itself...

Bartolotti house on Herengracht 170-172

Small fronts and deep houses. This had to do with the amount of tax that was levied based on the width of a property. Especially the merchants' houses had a lot of storage in the attic and cellar of their buildings.

The merchants wanted to outdo each other with the decorations on their gables. There are many different types of gables: Step gables, Bell gables, Neck gables which were either standard or elongated, Spout gables, Cornice gables with luxurious variations in the Louis 15th or 16th style and the Renaissance gables.

Additions such as tympans, pinnacles and special claws gave unusual details to a building.

A large number of these houses are now owned by the Hendrick de Keyser Society who takes care of restorations and then carefully chooses its tenants.

There is very little known about the builders and the original occupants of the houses. It is nearly impossible to trace the history of a house due to the lack of deeds.

The national register of properties was not initiated until the beginning of the 19th century.

The only records from those days are the tax lists. During several periods fireplace taxes were collected. The amount depended upon how many open fires, cooking areas and trading fires there were in the house.

There was also the so-called 'Heerengeld'(Gentlemen's taxes) which was collected for keeping servants. These registers give an insight as to who the previous owners or tenants were.

Brouwersgracht

During the second half of the 17th century the window became the most important element of the elegance of the gable. Windows divided into smaller windows with wooden rods replaced the leaded window panels.

Just before 1800 a larger division of the window became popular. Many of the cross windows were replaced by sliding windows.

If you look carefully you will notice that some of the canal houses have been restored to their original state. Other houses display the other variations.

Most of the Amsterdam gables were originally made from wood. In the Middle Ages the roofs were often made from straw or wooden planks fastened in a scale-like manner. Because of the fire hazardness, but also due to the prosperity during the 'Golden Age' many of these houses were altered or completely rebuilt.

Pavements were closed off with elegant wrought iron gates or a row of short stone piles. The pavement in front of the house was no longer space for general use or sales, but considered the bottom of the gable.

The 'Brewers Canal' forms the north-west border of the canal-network. It was dug much earlier than the other canals and therefor it played a vital role, being so near to the harbour, to the IJ and the Spaarne.

It is easy to understand where the name Brewers Canal comes from. The main activity along this canal was connected to the brewing of beer. After the canal was further dug out towards the west, the factories and warehouses became the centre of industry.

In the 1980's the storage houses on number 204 and 206 were refurbished for living accommodation. It is a lovely location to live. In the old days the other canals were where rich people lived and enjoyed tranquillity, because the Brouwersgracht was where polluting activities took place.

Products such as saltpetre, leather and whale-oil were processed and stored here.

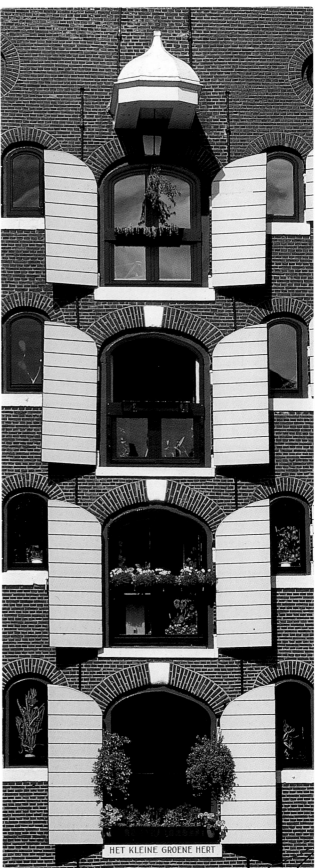

The Brouwersgracht has been through the transition of being a sombre and smelly place of industry to a popular residential area with the warehouses renovated to accommodate apartments and shops. The wooden shutters in front of the windows were there to protect the goods that were in storage. Warehouses can be recognized by their shutters.

The 'Slagthuis' is a complex of three neighbouring warehouses with Step gables. In 1894 it became destined for living accommodation. In the last century in Brouwersgracht 198, children of the poor went to school. Now it has cheap rental accommodation in it. The two big warehouses that stand on each side of the narrow one on numbers 204 - 206 used to store grain. Many young people live in the area which makes it a lively place to live.

HET KLEINE GROENE HERT

At the beginning of the 17th century the Zandhoek area (Sand Corner) was owned by the wealthy Reaal family. In 1645 the first premises were sold. Ten years later Mr. Frans Reaal sold the lots on the south side.

At number 4 (top photograph, middle) you can discover three personalized signs: St. Peter, Noachs Ark and S. Jan.

To give an impression of the prices for property and land in those days: on 9th May 1656 the property at number 4 was bought by C.P. Steiger, a bargeman, for 625 Dutch guilders.

There are many old warehouses in the Zandhoek area and all have been changed into modern apartments. The place where the Bloemgracht, the Brouwersgracht and the Prinsengracht come together is a very picturesque point.

Northern Church

Since the Noorderkerk was built it has hardly changed. This sober and solid church without any splendour came about due to the need for calvinistic place of worship in 1620.

The graveyard in front of the church later became the place for the market. On Mondays there is an ordinary market and a flee market. On Saturdays there is a market for ecological products held here.

Herengracht

The city of Amsterdam has actually been built on a former swamp area. In certain parts of the city the jerry-buildings are not in good condition anymore. To save costs, the amount of piles used to support buildings were halved.

The most expensive properties are the buildings that are properly supported and still stand straight. These houses are located along the canals.

Many Amsterdammers live on the canals and therefore have a lot to do with the quality of the water that is in the canals. The canals can be called 'clean'.

Until 1988, each night 600.000 m² of water was flushed through the canal system to. Because now only the house boats deposite into the canals directly, the flushings only take place four times per week. It is not advisable to dive to the bottom of the canal as there it is still polluted.

Herengracht

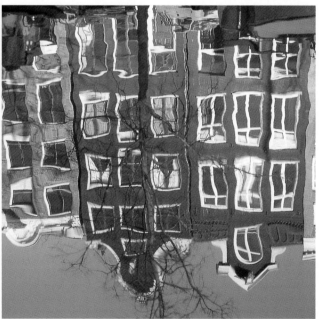

Keizersgracht

In the course of time the Herengracht was considered the most prestigious canal in Amsterdam. Very rich people lived there including the Mayor. Since 1926 the house at Herengracht number 502 is the official residence for the Mayor. This is where the Mayor still receives important foreign visitors.

The beautiful gables do not only reflect into the water, they are best admired from the water. When on a trip along the canals the guide will call the attention to the fact that the Mayor is at home, because his bicycle is 'parked against the tree'.

The Bartolotti house located at number 170-172 was built in 1615 by the well known Hendrick de Keyser. The person who commissioned the building of the double house with its red bricks and mountain stone was called Willem van den Heuvel. He had an ordinary name, but changed his name to that of his rich uncle: the Italian nobleman Bartolotti.

Herengracht

There are an unknown number of special stone tablets in Amsterdam. The oldest ones date back to the time that this harbour and merchants town was growing. In those days the houses did not have numbers and because many people could not read the stones formed a visual description of the people who lived there. A stone tablet was often also seen as a status symbol.

There are many different descriptions for the stone tablet: address-card or calling-card, advertisement stone, sign, religious expression, folklore or mythology, stone with family crests or mottos, etc.

Generally a stone tablet is made from a piece of natural stone with a relief picture carved out of it. This can be either coloured in or not.

Sometimes the picture has a text added and some tablets are only text. Fortunately many new stone tablets are made or old one are restored. The stone tablet is mostly shaped rectangular with the long sides horizontally. Very old tablets are nearly square.

There is a stone tablet on the Lindegracht that is very unusual. It shows a mirror imaged picture. This was not a mistake made by the stone mason, but a deliberate commission. This way the occupants of the house could see the correct picture reflected in the water.

Around 1600 the cartouche shape with scrolls became fashionable. The Italian 'cartoccio' means rolled up cardboard. A cartouche is an ornament, mostly an arched stone with scrolls.

There are stone tablets shaped like a niche. These are remainders from the time that small holy statues were place in them. These were mostly on street corners.

Stone tablets either have only texts or text as a subscript to a picture. Motto's were sometimes written on the tablets and made to resemble a ribbon.

Some of the stone tablets with pictures are real works of art. Unfortunately most of the texts are disappointing. Often the letters are not placed correctly and they have spelling mistakes. When many of these stone tablets were made the rules of grammar were hardly known.

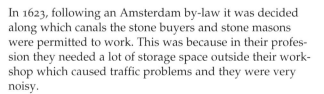

In 1623, following an Amsterdam by-law it was decided along which canals the stone buyers and stone masons were permitted to work. This was because in their profession they needed a lot of storage space outside their workshop which caused traffic problems and they were very noisy.

The Jordaan area has always been known as that part of the city centre where the social life centered around the pubs. The Jordaan is situated between the Lijnbaansgracht, the Brouwersgracht, the Prinsengracht and the Leidsestraat. Between 1609 and 1614, the canals and streets were built on existing polder roads. This way of building created an area with unique topographical character.

Although many people from the Jordaan have moved away to towns like Almere, there is still much of the old atmosphere left. The typical Jordaan style of having cats and plants behind the windows, spy-mirrors to watch everything happening on the street from the comfort of the your own armchair, pigeon-lofts and fishing clubs, all this still is part of living in the Jordaan.

The emigrants and current population often meet in the local pubs. The sense of nostalgia of 'the old days' is a driving force. The people in the Jordaan are good-natured and sentimental by heart.

This is demonstrated by a strong sense of neighbourly helpfulness and community spirit, and also because of the strong preference of communal singing of songs laden with sentimental texts.

It is fair to say that the street-organ originated in the Jordaan.

The Perlee family were famous Jordaan street-organs builders. Women dressed in flannel skirts and men wearing smock waltzed gracefully to the tune of the street-organ. The dance was mostly performed with one hand behind their back.

It is uncertain where the name 'Jordaan' originates. The two historians Meijer and Beets have tried to compare this part of Amsterdam with the Jordan land mentioned in the Bible.

The oldest part of the Jordaan is located along the Karthuizerstraat. Already in 1394(!) the Karthuizer monastery was built. In 1577 the Sea-Beggars completely destroyed it. The current Karthuizerhof, also known as 'House-sitting Widows Courtyard', dates back to 1650.

The (rental) houses were renovated by the Amsterdam Housing Corporation in 1986. The plans by the Amsterdam council for new housing are met by supporters and opposers. Despite depopulation (around 718.000 inhabitants in 1998) and the fact that thousands of houses that have been built in the meantime, there are still over 32.000 house-hunters on the urgency list in Amsterdam.

The former KNSM island is the location for the building of new houses. The properties already on the island used to belong to the KNSM (Royal Dutch Steamboat Company). From 1902 this company ran regular services to the Dutch Indies and the Near East.

Following the closure of the KNSM, and many discussions, it was decided to build houses on the island. The city architectural plan by Prof. Jo Coenen would be used.

The project was to be supervised by Prof. Tjeerd Dijkstra. The designers envisioned a 'Quality of the open space'. The neighbours were very doubtful. For example, an action committee called the 'Suspended Sister' saved a group of seven trees from being cut down. The trees were considered essential to the general atmosphere of the island.

The action group that lobbied about the trees itself was named 'The Seven Sisters'. Since July 1998 there is an action committee called 'Can Not Get Worse' that is active in rallying for liveability for the island. The KNSM island has now nearly completely built-on.

The Java Island, Borneokade and Sporenburg locations are next. There are also plans to create artificial islands in the IJ. These will be near the Diemerzeedijk. These islands would accommodate another 18.000 houses.

Building on artificial islands is not new to Amsterdammers. Examples are Kattenburg, Wittenburg and Zeeburg. Now IJburg will be added.

The Westerkerk is the largest and most monumental Reformed Church in Holland. The tower of the Westerkerk lost its status as highest tower when the Rembrandt tower was built. However the Westerkerk is the church with the most songs written about it.

The top was a gift from Emperor Maximilian. The imperial crown is beautifully decorated with 870 glass pearls.

As the emperor had not been crowned by the Pope, he was not allowed to donate the crown to the church. This problem was solved by using the crown of emperor Rudolf II as an example.

The church was designed by Hendrick de Keyser who placed the first stone in 1620. He died in 1621 and his son Pieter continued his work. Pieter altered the design a little so it looks more classicistic. Of course the tower houses a Hemony carillon.

Interior of the Westerkerk

The interior of the Westerkerk is sober as well as impressive. There are no mausoleums or sepulchral monuments. The fact that Rembrandt lies buried in this church is only mentioned on a simple memorial stone in one of the pillars. The exact spot is not even indicated.

Other well known people that have their final resting place in the Westerkerk are Rembrandt's son Titus, the publisher and printer Joan Blaeu and the distiller Jan Bols. In 1966 our present Queen Beatrix and Prince Claus had their marriage blessed in the Westerkerk.

The house where Anne Frank lived when she was in hiding from 1942 onwards is one of the most visited houses in Amsterdam. For over two years she, her family and friends lived in the back part of the house.

The entrance was hidden behind a book case. After two years they were betrayed, arrested and taken away. Only Anne's father survived the war. The Anne Frank Foundation looks after the house and carries out Anne's ideals.

Book case and hiding place

Anne Frank

At the end of the last century the canal-system was altered to make way for a busy traffic-artery: the Raadhuisstraat. This street is dominated by the shopping-arcade which was designed by A.L. van Gendt and commissioned by an insurance company called 'De Utrecht'.

The crocodiles and other animals of prey carved in stone are possibly there to inspire unsuspecting passers-by to purchase insurance against the dangers in life. The White House built in the Jugendstil style was also commissioned by the insurance company.

To enable the tram to cross the canals, the street had to be widened between the Jordaan and the Royal Palace. The works involved with this have been painted by George Breitner. The painter and photographer (1857-1923) has captured life and work in Amsterdam in many different ways. His workshop and home were at Prinseneiland 24b. In 1898 this accommodation was offered to him by the builder C.J. Maks in exchange for painting lessons for his son. Breitner developed a northern form of impressionism with big shapes, a coarse touch of the brush and without much detail.

Over the latest centuries many painters have visited Amsterdam. During the 18th century especially French artists such as Manet and Picasso came. Claude Monet also regularly travelled to Holland to be inspired during the 1870's. He has painted the Zuiderkerk in Amsterdam, seen from the Groenburgwal.

Another well known typical Amsterdam scene, the Herb Market on the Singel, was painted by the 17th century painter Gabriël Metsu.

Westerkerk with the Gay Monument in the foreground

View of the Bartolotti house with the Westerkerk in the background, seen from the Singel

Prinsengracht

Entrance gate to the Amsterdam Historical Museum on the Kalverstraat

Just a short walk from the Dam you will find the Amsterdam Historical Museum. The building used to be the Common Orphanage and between 1520 and 1960 over 15.000 orphans lived here. The museum has twenty halls, one of them is the Governors Hall.

The Schuttersgalerij (Citizen Soldiers Gallery) is the only public museum street in the world. The paintings that hang there are so large they can not hang anywhere else in the museum.

Citizen Soldiers Gallery

Both entrance gates to the museum are finely decorated. (Above: seen from the Luciensteeg and bottom: seen from the Kalverstraat).

Before arriving at the actual entrance to the museum you pass through the impressive 'meisjesbinnenplaats' ('girls courtyard'). There is also a boys courtyard with the well known statues of David and Goliath. These statues originate from a private garden on the Prinsengracht.

St. Luciensteeg

As soon as you walk through the gate of the Begijnhof you leave the bustle of the city behind you and step into an oasis of peace. Walking in the serenity of the 'hofje' (courtyard) it is very easy to imagine how the women that wanted to lead a religious life lived. Without having to go into a convent they could live here away from the world.

After the Reformation their properties were not disowned as the houses were not owned by the church, but by the Begijn people themselves. Behind the gable of number 29-31, there you will find hidden the St. Joannes and St. Ursula church.

This Miracle- or Begijnhof chapel dates back to 1671 and for many people it is considered to be the start and finish of the 'Holy Procession' that keeps tradition of the Miracle alive. The chapel is also a popular place for Catholic marriage blessings.

In the centre of the Begijnhof stands the Gothic Church which was built in 1400 and allocated to the Reformers in 1578.

The monument had been standing empty for years and later served as a warehouse. In the 17th century, after extensions, the building was used as a church for the English Presbyterian community in Amsterdam.

The stone tablets in the Begijnhof depict the flight out of Egypt, martyrs and men of Emmaüs. There are two more entrances besides the main entrances. From the Kalverstraat, the Begijnsteeg leads to a small gate and there is a gate to the Spui.

There are symbols of a cockerel and a dog that rush towards the Spui along the gate. These were to make clear that no men were allowed to be in the courtyard at night.

During the 17th and 18th century the houses in the Begijnhof were given new gables. The house at number 34 has a wooden gable, as was common at the end of the 14th century. This 'Wooden House' is one of the two oldest houses in Amsterdam. The other house is on the Zeedijk. The front and rear gables are made of wood and the interior is built up using a Gothic wooden house skeleton.

Oldest house in Amsterdam

The Begijnhof is very well maintained and restored. It could feel like walking onto a filmset.

The courtyard resemble a small village with its old houses, church and a round park with very old trees. The activities of the city is hardly noticeable. Due to the charity of private people and organizations these houses, are one the first old people's home in Amsterdam.

In 1672 the rich merchant Jeremias van Raey commissioned the architect Adriaan Dortsman to design and build two adjoining houses. The staircase is decorated with the gods that symbolised the goods that he traded: Mars, Minerva, Vulcanus and Ceres stood for Weapons, Iron and Grain. The right part of the large building is now the Van Loon Museum. Its first inhabitant was Ferdinand Bol, the best known pupil of Rembrandt. In 1753 the house was bought by physician Abraham van Hagen who was married to Catharina Trip, daughter of Mayor Trip.

It was Van Hagen who collected the 18th century interior that can been seen today. The beautiful brass banister decorated with the names of the Hagen and Trip families is spectacular.

In 1884 the house was bought by the governors family Van Loon. This family lived here till 1945. In 1973 the last male Van Loon in line, Maurits van Loon, opened the house to the public following a long restoration. The interior shows how rich the Van Loon family lived.

There is a hidden garden behind the house that can be seen from the room that overlooks the garden. It has been designed in a formal style with trimmed hedges, rosaries and a monumental beech. The garden is sealed by the classicist gable of the coach-house.

The 18th century period rooms have about 80 family portraits dating between 1600 right up to the present day. The rooms are filled with authentic furniture, carpets, silverware, porcelain and family memorabilia. In the basement you can visit the kitchen.

The unique collection of family portraits tells the history of the Van Loon family and at the same time shows the development of the art of portrait-painting over the past few centuries.

The family had themselves painted by the most prominent painters such as Santvoort, Nicolaas Maes and Hodges.

Highlights are two group-portraits by a pupil of Frans Hals, Jan Miense Molenaer. 'Wedding of Willem van Loon and Margaretha Bas' and 'Four ages or the five senses' are two painting filled with symbols that refer to worldly wisdom and conjugal fidelity. The romantic double portrait by Tischbein dates back to the 18th century.

The photographs depict the life of Thora van Loon-Egidius who was a representative for Queen Wilhelmina in Amsterdam.

The still strategically located Munt Tower (meaning Coin Tower)dates back to the Middle Ages. The Munt Tower has a passage and, just like the Montelbaans Tower, was part of the fortifications of Amsterdam. Two other towers are gone. It used to be used as a town entrance (Regulierspoort).

The building derives its name from the fact that golden and silver coins were striken here since 1672. This activity actually only took place for a short period, during the second half of the 17th century, but the building has kept the name.

In 1620 the 41 metres high tower received a new rooftop. The square in front of the tower originally was called Schapenmarkt (sheepmarket).

Actually it is not a square, but a bridge from the Singel to the Amstel as described elsewhere. The official name during the 19th century was 'Sophia Plein'.
Everyone calls it the Munt Tower and so that is the name for it today.

Muntplein (square)

Munt Tower

Around the corner from the Muntplein lies the Rokin with very special buildings. At number 112 the Company Arti et Amicitiae is located. This is a nearly 160 year old society for design artists. It is not a museum or gallery, but a 'laboratorium for creative minds'.

The monuments on numbers 145-147 were created in Dutch classicistic style by the architect Philips Vingboons.

The first stock exchange was located on the Rokin. In 1611 it was opened and mainly used to trade goods and spices from all over the world. In those days trading in stocks and shares was only a very small part of the exchange's business and the money and capital market.

Rokin

Rokin/Old Turfmarket

There is a lot of traffic on the canals. Besides the sight-seeing boats that take about an hour, there are alternatives such as the Museum boat. This boat has seven stops and travels past sixteen museums, several shopping centres and places to eat and drink.

There is also an Artis Express. You get on board and are directly taken to the oldest zoo in Holland. Returning to your place of departure can be by alternative routes.

Several boat companies offer Dinner-cruises, romantic Candle-light trips and Business tours.

If the group is between 8 and 25 people there are special water-taxi's. These can be hired by the hour and can take the passengers to places in Amsterdam that larger boats can not reach.

Sight-seeing boats travel along the canals and through the harbour and cover an

Munt Tower

There is a slight resemblance between the Zuiderkerk and the Westerkerk. They were both designed by Hendrick de Keyser. The view of the tower, when looking at it from the Groenburgwal, is considered to be the most beautiful of anywhere in the city.

The Zuiderkerk, built in 1614, was the first church built after the Reformation and originally was called the Sint-Jans Church. The Reformed wanted to do away with Roman superstition and renamed it the Zuiderkerk.

Inside the church are the graves of Hendrick de Keyser, the three eldest children of Rembrandt and the painter Ferdinand Bol.

During the famine winter of 1944-45, the dead were brought into the church. The inside of the church then resembled a mortuary. The dead were laid there temporarily as there was not enough wood available to make coffins for the victims of hunger and illness.

Zuiderkerk

*House on the three
canals*

According to the inscription on the bell made in 1511, 'the great Salvator wakes the living, cries for the dead and breaks the lightning'. This bell was delivered to the Zuiderkerk in 1659.

Vivos voco, mortuos plango, vulgura frango is Schiller's motto for his 'Lied von der Glocke' (Song of the bell) and is also engraved. This large bell was cast by Jasper Moer. There are other bells in the tower and these come from the house of François Hemony.

*Old Manhouse
Gate*

Stopera

Initially there were not enough funds to carry out the award-winning design for a town-hall. The international competition for city hall design was won by the architect Holzbauer from Vienna. Not until it was decided to combine the townhall project with an opera house did the plans come together and the Stopera emerged. Life in the Amsterdam city centre was disrupted for years because of the building of the Stopera and the underground metro. After the opening of the complex in 1986, everything went back to normal.

For centuries the standard for all measurements of height in the Netherlands has been the Normaal Amsterdams Peil (Normal Amsterdam Level). This foundation for measurements used to be located in a sinister ditch at the Dam. Now can be seen at the end of a covered street in the Stopera-complex.

The gauge is not just a symbol of the N.A.P, but the actual standard level. The townhall annex music theatre on the Amstel is a complex of covered passages with an underground, but people-friendly, parking area and the grand café Dantzig. At the time when the townhall was being built it caused a lot of resistance in the area. An old neighbourhood had to be demolished for the project. Additionally not everyone liked the design of the Stopera. Also the project was much more expensive than initially was decided upon.

Now the complex is more or less accepted. Seen from the water the Stopera does not seem out of place on the Staalkade.

The townhall and the music theatre operate to everyone's satisfaction, which was the main objective.

This complex has confirmed that it is possible to integrate an old city structure and modernisation in harmony.

Staalkade   *N.A.L. Gauge in Stopera*

Everything you could possibly want, you can find on the largest flea-market in Holland, at Waterlooplein. The market is situated between the Stopera and the beautiful houses on the Jodenbreestraat. Rich and poor jews from Spain, Portugal, Germany, Russia and Poland ran the colourful market from around 1813 onwards. The atmosphere of the market as it was before the Second World War has never returned. The diversity of goods on offer is still unbelievable.

It is a very popular market for collectors. Also young couples find pieces for their interior.

During the 'Flower Power' period the hippies were able to find clothing from their grandmother's time. Today still clothing forms a large part of the market.

Mozes and Aäron Church

The original Mozes and Aäronchurch was a Catholic clandestine church located in a house near the rear side of the current church. It was in the Jodenbreestraat and called: Moyses. The building next to it was called Aäron and was later added to Moyses. The current building was built in a Neo-Classicistic style by T.F. Suys in 1841. It is now used for social and cultural manifestations.

The Willet-Holthuijsen Museum is located in a double house on the Herengracht number 605 dating back to 1687. Many different rich Amsterdam families have come by the property through marriages, legacies and inheritances. These were Jacob Hop, Isabella Hooft, Jean Deutz, Willem Gideon Deutz. In 1855 Pieter Gerard Holthuijsen owned it. He was a glass merchant and coal importer. His daughter, Sandra Louisa Geertruida, married Abraham Willet, who was a collector.

Around 1860 alterations were made to the house and in 1888 Abraham Willet died. In 1895 his widow donated the property, including its contents, to the city of Amsterdam with the condition that it would be open to the public under the name Willet-Holthuijsen.

In 1962 the house became a museum that was dedicated to the interior and belongings of rich aristocrats. The original legacy was enlarged with items from heirlooms of the Amsterdam governors family Backer. The double house has five windows and was built according to a symmetric plan. Each floor has its specific theme.

The rooms show the styles of furnishing that were fashionable in the 18th and 19th century. Sometimes the styles are mixed.

Servants quarters, the cellar and a provisions room were located in the basement. The kitchen is a copy of an 18th century kitchen with a granite sink, a pipe system and mainly 18th century utilities from other houses.

The landing of the English and Russian troops at Bergen in 1799 are depicted on the tiled tableau from the 19th century.

The dinner service dates back to the 17th, 18th and 19th century.

The ground floor houses the reception rooms. The drawing-rooms and dining-rooms are located around the central hall.

The ball-room, the conservatory and dining-room on the ground floor have been renovated.

Different collections can be seen in the rooms on the first floor.

The room dedicated to special occasions such as costumed balls or music recitals, has a very special and beautifully decorated mantlepiece. In 1865 Abraham Willet personally ordered this room to be furnished in Louis 16th style. Three guests wearing historic outfits are 'present'.

The round room on the ground floor has a view of the garden. The panelling in this room are according to the fashion in the last century: pale green. The small table in the centre of the room is decorated with French inlaid work with

music instruments motif. The enormous garden of the Willet-Holthuijsen Museum can be seen from the Amstelstraat. This is unique in Amsterdam. This large French garden used to facilitate a coach-house and horse-stables and was laid-out according to the Dutch fashion of the 18th century. In the garden you will find not only a sun-dial, but the usual statues such as Mercury (God of Trade), Flora (Goddess of flowers) and Pomina (Goddess of gardens).

The canal house on Herengracht number 605 will surely lure you to want to come in and visit the authentic beautiful mansion. The richly decorated Rococo entrance is exquisite.

The period rooms, the paintings, prints and the collection of glass-work do give a good impression of the living conditions of the wealthy in the previous century.

Near the end of the 16th century a square piece of swamp-land is raised. Two streets divide the land into 4 parts. This is where the area was created where after the year 1600 many refugee jews from Portugal and jewish immigrants from Middle-Europe came to make their home. This is where the Jodenbreestraat is. The Rembrandt house is on number 4 which the house where Rembrandt lived and worked from 1639 to 1658.

Rembrandt lived on the ground floor. His studio was on the first floor and has been restored to its original state. His pupils, one of them being Ferdinand Bol, occupied the second floor. In the 88 years since the museum was opened it's collection has grown to be almost a complete compilation of Rembrandt's graphical work.

The collection comprises about 250 etchings (biblical representations, landscapes, portraits and self-portraits), a few drawings and a small collections of paintings from artists that worked next to Rembrandt. These were mainly pupils and predecessors. He had some hard times when he lived in the house on the Jodenbreestraat. His wife Saskia died in 1642 and out of his four children only his son Titus lived. Commissions from his maecenas Jan Six made it possible for him to survive.

The street on the Jodenbreestraat has changed enormously, especially during the seventies. But the house on number 4, the house where the biggest painter of the Golden Age, miller's son Rembrandt van Rijn lived still stands. Rembrandt was born in Leiden in 1606.

In an area where many jew lived the years of economic recession were very noticeable. Rembrandt worked in a multi-cultural atmosphere filled with different cultures, languages and religions. He did not have to look far for models: shabby neighbours, wealthy people inspired him for his religious paintings. His graving-tools, brushes and pallets captured the images of the bearded jews from Eastern Europe or the noblemen jews from Portugal.

Rembrandt made hundreds of self-portraits, more than any other painter. These portraits display an enormous range of human emotions. In one he is serious, in another happy or soft, proud, self-confident, vain or hurt.

Self-portrait leaning on a banister (1639)

Portrait of a beggar (1630)

Dutch landscape

St. Antonie Lock

The water-level in the Amsterdam canals is regulated by a number of locks and sluices. The Sint Antonie Lock in the Oude Schans has an old fashioned charm and is still used regularly for transport over water.

In the far distance, even further than the Montelbaan Tower you can see the Kikkerbilsluis. A little further down this connects the eastern dock to the IJ.

Montelbaan Tower

The Montelbaan Tower was to built to be part of the fortifications of Amsterdam. Since 1878 it houses the City Water Office.

In 1512 the tower was erected to protect the nearby shipyards, the Lastage. The ships that were part of the trade- and war-fleet were built and repaired here.

The city council were afraid of raids from unsavoury armies.

The pretty top-part of the tower was designed by the architect Hendrick de Keyser and was completed in 1606. The tower was then 48 metres high.

In 1648 the Munster Treaty was signed, meaning the end of the Eighty Years of War with Spain. The shipyards then moved to more spacious locations. The empty docks were then used to build nice mansions for the new generation of merchants, who had brought prosperity to the city. The 17th century in Holland is not called the 'Golden Age' for nothing.

Montelbaan Tower

Among others a replica of the V.O.C. ship 'Amsterdam' (original was built in 1749) is moored in front of the Maritime Museum. The Museum originally was built to be 's Lands Zeemagazijn (warehouse for the Admiralty). It is possible to take boat trips on the historic steamship 'Christiaan Brunnings' (1901) or the lifeboat 'Insulinde' (1926).

On the Oostenburg island, which is nearby, the merchants of the Verenigd Oost-Indische Company (United East Indies Company) built their own shipyards and warehouses.

Maritime Museum

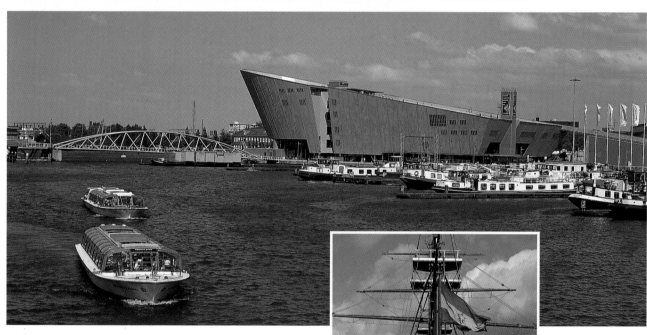

New Metropolis

Besides a collection of old models of ships, sea-maps, paintings and a unique royal barge, the museum has number of small shops that will please model builders and collectors.

Situated near the Maritime Museum you will find the New Metropolis. It is located on top of the IJ tunnel and was built by the Italian architect Renzo Piano. It has the shape of a giant's ship.

VOC ship ' Amsterdam'

The shipyard 't Kromhout is one of the most special industrial monuments in Amsterdam. The original shipyard (around 1760) was taken over by the Goedkoop family in 1867. Seven years later the last wooden ship was left the quay. In that year Goedkoop acquired a steam-engine and went into steel. Twice the shipyard expanded, in 1888 and 1899. The foundation for the world famous Kromhout engines (on petroleum with magnetic ignition) came from here in 1904.

In 1967 the activities of the yard came to an end and there was a threat of demolition. Fortunately it was prevented and the shipyard gained recognition as a national monument. Presently there is a 't Kromhout museum and a part of the yard is still used as a shipyard.

Skinny Bridge over the river Amstel

It can be assumed that in 1275 the place called 'Amstelredam' already was a community with primarily fishermen. It is not known when the very first people made their home on the spot where later the dam was made in the river Amstel. The National Monument is now on that precise location.

Carré Theatre on the Amstel

There is a legend that tells the story of two men and a dog that were shipwrecked from their Koggeship on that spot. There they found a piece of dry and fertile land and started a settlement there. The men, the dog and the Koggeship are often depicted in the old civic crest of the capital. It is quiet an experience to walk along or sail over the still very lively river Amstel.

Staalkade

Arriving in Amsterdam from Amstelveen you will see beautiful country houses along a wide stretch of water. The river is wide and busy with ships even all the way into to the heart of the city. The theatre Carré dominates along the river. We have elaborated in another part of this book about this theatre.

Another 'crown jewel' along the river is the monumental 'Amstel Hotel Inter-Continental'. This grand hotel was built in 1867 and was fantastically renovated in 1992.

Bridge over the Nieuwe Heren-gracht   *House-boats on the Amstel*

Along the Amstel there are many different house-boats. Many boat owners are adventurers or financially less fortunates who the city of Amsterdam can not offer affordable accommodation. Till now the city council has tolerated their presence.

Amstel

Skinny Bridge

The Skinny Bridge across the river Amstel is probably the most photographed bridge in Amsterdam. This bridge is lit by thousands of light-bulbs at night during the Summer months. The bridge is named after the sisters Mager (Skinny) who owned land on the other side of the river.

In 1671 they were given a bridge by the city council. The current double draw-bridge was built in 1840 and restored in 1934. A little further down the river is the theatre Carré. This was built to function as a circus in the last century. Now, any self- respecting performer must have played this theatre at least once in his or her life. Either in a musical, cabaret show or as a soloist.

Panorama of the 'Amstel'

Skinny Bridge

Amstel Hotel

Near the financial, shopping and theatre areas, along the riverbank you will find the Amstel Hotel. It is an architecturally magnificent piece of work. The hotel is a monument and dates back to 1866. It has 79 rooms, terraces, an excellent restaurant and a piano bar. It is part of the Inter-Continental Group.

Amsterdam also plays an important role on the financial market. On national level Amsterdam is the centre for the financial market and internationally it can be considered mediocre.

Not only the head offices of the Netherlands Bank and the Financial Branch Office are located in Amsterdam. The Stock Exchange, the Insurance Exchange and the Option Exchange are here too.

Head office Netherlands Bank

Reguliersgracht

The spot as shown above is where all the sight-seeing boats slow down a little. Exactly here is where you can see seven stone bridges all around you.

Johan Rudolf Thorbecke was a statesman who lived from 1798 till 1872. He can be considered as a progressive-historical, anti-ideological and pragmatic man.

He played a very important role in the development of the constitution in the Netherlands.

Thorbecke

Rembrandtplein

Holland's most famous painter Rembrandt van Rijn watches over 'his' square. He stands surrounded by greenery and in the middle of a hasty and stone world built for pleasure. On nice summer days sun lovers lie on the grass around Rembrandt.

The Rembrandtplein (square) is lined with many different hotels, terraces and places to go out. The 'Royal Café De Kroon' has a special story. It was named after the crowning of Queen Wilhelmina in the year that it was built, 1898. During the war it lost most of its (jewish) clientele and had to close in 1950.

The café-restaurant did not retrieve its old grandeur until 1990. De Kroon has a very unique antique interior, a mixture of Louis 16th furniture and an English Library bar. Next to De Kroon the same owners run a large discotheque called 'Escapade'.

Another interesting place to go out is 'Schiller'. The property dates back to 1860 and has recently been renovated in the Art Nouveau style. Terraces on the square are frequently visited by writers and poets of the city.

At a right angle to the Rembrandtplein is the Thorbeckeplein. This too is a social square with many places to go out.

Rembrandt

The square near the Munt Tower is actually very unusual. The water from the river Amstel is in connection with water of the Singel and therefor flows underneath the square. It is also a very complicated crossing for trams, cars, bicycles and pedestrians.

From the Muntplein you can walk through the Kalverstraat towards the Dam and through the Reguliersbreestraat it will take you straight to the places to go out on the Rembrandsplein.

Behind the Munt Tower and along the Singel you will find the flower market. The market is a sea of colourful flowers and plants and is open all year round. The plants and flowers are delivered by the largest flower auction in the world, in Aalsmeer. Naturally, Amsterdammers buy flowers and plants to put in front of their windows or next to their front doors and to liven up their houses. Flower bulbs are mainly bought by tourists as a colourful souvenir from Holland.

Japanese tourists especially enjoy the sunflowers that the painter Van Gogh loved so much. He seems to be even better known in Japan than his own country.

It is not only the inhabitants of Amsterdam that add to the natural colourfulness of their city by displaying their personal taste in flowers or plants. The city council makes sure that there is a lot of public greenery all over Amsterdam. In Holland, Amsterdam is the city with the most trees.

It has a long tradition of much green in the city. A 17th century traveller once wondered whether he was in 'a forest in the town' or in 'a town in the forest'. Some of the trees in Amsterdam have a monument status. Since 1525 these monuments are protected by covenants.

Amsterdam has about a quarter of a million trees, 25 parks and 15 percent of the city area (300 hectares) is green. During the 19th century the parks were laid out without planning. During the following century the planning department was responsible for inner city greenery. The Amsterdamse Bos (Amsterdam Forrest) was a planned greenery. On busy days around 80.000 people come to enjoy the park.

There is a collaboration between private and public greenery within the Singel canal area: the garden.

Gardens of the houses along the Keizersgracht, Herengracht and Prinsengracht seen as part of the city and considered monuments of culture.

Behind many of the houses along the canals are charming and beautifully designed garden houses. They can not been seen from the street, but give the occupants a lovely view into their gardens. The courtyards also offer a way to enjoy the oasis of natural tranquillity within the city.

Brouwersgracht

Even though the greenery in Amsterdam is completely organized, any personal favourite flowers and plants or trees will definitely add to a general atmosphere of friendly living.

Reguliersgracht

Brouwersgracht

Brandts Rusthofje

From the beginning of the 17th century till 1900 there were 51 courtyards created in Amsterdam. Seven have disappeared completely and of the 44 left over a number have been thoroughly renovated. These courtyards were there to house 'lone women, mostly over 50 years, not wealthy but of impeccable reputation'. It was often necessary for the women to be a member of a certain religious community (Reformed, Lutheran, Baptist, etc.).

There were no specifically male courtyards, and only a few houses were meant for couples.

Courtyards were mostly started by rich people, often without children. One example is the Van Brandtshofje along the Nieuwe Keizersgracht 28-44. Christoffel Brandts had made his fortune in trading with Russia. Tsar Peter the Great elevated him to nobility in 1717 and from then he was allowed to call himself 'Van'. He remained a bachelor and had the courtyard built in 1732-1733. Another 'distinguished' courtyard is the Corvershof.

Corvershof along the Nieuwe Keizersgracht

Entrance to the Zonshofje along the Prinsengracht

Rozenhofje

The small houses were built around the courts to form a U- or and L-shape. The rectangular complex had a bleaching field in the centre (now it is mostly a pleasant garden). In principle the courtyards are accessible to the public, but unfortunately it happens more and more often that the entrance can found to be locked.

Often the rooms are rented to students and other young people. There are very few courtyards left that have rent free accommodation.

Not all the courtyards can be found or recognized as such. They have either a doorway along the street or from canal and are located and hidden behind other houses.

These cottages were an early form of care for the elderly and social housing. They catered for the old and poor people. Most courtyards have a water-pump with a lantern.

The governor's room was mainly located above the entrance on the first floor. It often contained a luxurious interior which was and is in enormous contrast to the very sober houses.

City Playhouse

The best way to describe the Leidseplein is 'the place to be in Holland for nightlife and fun'.

This is where you find nice pubs, terraces, many places to eat. Around the square there are a number of special buildings such as the City Playhouse and the 'Hotel American' built in Neo-Gothic style. The hotel was built in 1882. It has 188 very modern rooms, but the café still carries an atmosphere of the turn of the century. Writers and poets frequent the café American. Sculptors have always met in the café's Eilder and Reijnders.

Leidseplein

Paradiso is a worldwide known place for young people to go out. It used to be a church. Now it holds very busy pop concerts.

Like on many squares in Amsterdam, you will find street artists and traders from many different countries performing and selling on the Leidseplein. The artists are often very amusing and musical. Sometimes they perform just for fun, but some see it as a way to earn a little extra money or possibly extent their stay in Amsterdam.

Max Euweplein

Holland Casino

Many real Amsterdammers will reminisce about the old wooden Lido building. This multifunctional entertainments location had to make way for the Holland Casino. Now this impressive building is considered to be one of the most modern in the world.

The colourful glass dome above the gambling-room is rather striking.

At the Casino you can play French Roulette, American Roulette, Black Jack, Caribbean Studpoker, Sic Bo, Big Wheel, Poker and Punto Banco. A visit to the bustling Jackpot Club or one of the four international Bars can be recommended. A stylish restaurant and a brasserie are also located in the building.

Vondelpark

This park first used to be called 'Riding and walking park' and then 'Nieuwe Park' (new park). With the unveiling of the statue of the Dutch poet Joost van den Vondel came its final name: 'Vondel park'.

In the 19th century it was customary to lay-out a park resembling the style of an English landscape. Over the years many changes have been made to the recreational park, but is has maintained its original romantic style. The oldest tree in Amsterdam is in this park. It is a one hundred year old black poplar that stands 35 metres high and has a circumference of nearly 6 metres.

The Amsterdam Patroness welcomes visitors at the Stadhouderskade entrance of this multi-functional park.

Statue of Joost van den Vondel

A variety of good or loud music can be enjoyed in the world famous concert-hall, the theatres or disco's. On the streets and squares of Amsterdam you can enjoy the music from the many typical Dutch street-organs. In Amsterdam these organs are called 'Pierementen'.

The bagpipe player shown on the photograph does not come from Scotland, but is an original Amsterdammer.

It seems that specially during the summer months many holiday-makers from all over the world want to play their instruments in Amsterdam. Classical music, pop, folklore or jazz are performed on the streets either for fun or to finance the visit to Amsterdam.

When strolling along the canals it is understandable that you would want to take a look inside these houses with their beautiful gables. In some cases it is definitely possible. The Anne Frank House is situated at the Prinsengracht number 266, near the Westertoren.

Museum Willet-Holthuijsen (Herengracht 366) is a house with beautiful period rooms and a fantastic 18th century city garden.

Museum Van Loon (Keizersgracht 672). This house was lived in by the Van Loon family until 1945 and the interior has been restored to its original state. It has a very impressive collection of paintings and furniture from the 18th century. The Biblical Museum and the Theatre Institute are also located in historical canal houses. Amsterdam can boast a grand total of 40 museums.

The names Reguliersstraat, Reguliersbreestraat, Reguliersdwarsstraat and Reguliersgracht are all located in Amsterdam. It is not clear why the people who named these streets used the name Regulier so often. 'Regulier' means regular, orderly and alive according to monastic rule.

Staalkade

Reguliersgracht

Herengracht

Leidsegracht

The city centre of Amsterdam is sometimes called the 'Venice of the North'. It has around 90 islands, divided by about 100 kilometres of canal and linked together by about 400 stone bridges ('locks').

The part of Amsterdam that was built during the Middle Ages was enclosed by a moat (now the Singel). The following circles built around it were: the Herengracht, Keizersgracht and Prinsengracht.

Herengracht/Reguliersgracht

In 1875 the architect P.J.H. Cuypers was appointed Master Builder for the Rijks Museum buildings. He also designed the largest museum in the Netherlands: the Rijksmuseum. The construction of the building has a distinctive Neo-Gothic style and is ornamented in a typical Dutch renaissance style.

Cuypers built the Neo-Gothic building with a steep tower from his Catholic tradition. He had a lot of experience with restoring Catholic churches.

When King Willem III saw the Rijksmuseum, he exclaimed: 'I will never set foot in this monastery'. The design had already been changed to comply with the wishes of the Reformed. They had wanted the pointed arches to be changed into vaulted arches.

The Rijksmuseum as well as the Central Station were both designed by Cuypers and both have a very broad front. The museum's walls depict the history of the Dutch arts.

In the heart of the Rijksmuseum, in the honourary gallery, hangs the Nightwatch by Rembrandt from 1642. The original name for the painting was 'This Company of Captain Cocq'.

At the time of this painting the great Dutch Master's style was already ahead of his peers in the Golden Age.

Although he was well appreciated and had many work commissions, during his lifetime he did not enjoy the reputation of being one of the world's most genius painters in history. When the Nightwatch was just painted there was a lot of criticism. The way in which the scene with the Company is painted definitely looks somewhat unusual.

The Company of Captain Cocq was one of the many citizen solderies that after a certain moment in history only gathered for banquets and parades.

The citizen soldiers originated from the civic duties the citizens of Amsterdam had to help defend the city. In 1578 each town district in Amsterdam had their own Company,

lead on by a Captain. The Captain was head of the area and was assisted by three lieutenants and three sergeants.

Later these citizen militia became shooting clubs. The shooting ranges, so-called 'Doelen' were later extended and more and more used for banquets and functions.

The soldiers were ordinary citizens and enjoyed a certain respect from the other citizens during the time of the Companies. The ranks of officers were only filled by members of the large patrician families. The social differences within the military hierarchy were clearly expressed in their dress and weaponry. This can be seen on the enormous paintings that the Companies commissioned to decorate the Doelen.

In 1813 the Companies ended without honour as the result of the decadency of the parties and festivities.

The very best painters, such as Rembrandt but also Van der Helst and Hals have made a great number of paintings in which these men are immortalized wearing their full outfits and enjoying themselves at the dining-table.

This is one the self-portraits of Van Gogh, painted during his 'explosive' period when his brightly coloured and passionate paintings developed. During his 'dark' period he painted for example 'the Potato Eaters'. After his 'dark' period Van Gogh encountered impressionism in Paris.

In 1888 Van Gogh lived in the Provence where the signs of his nervous disease were noticeable. A year later he went to live in a sanitorium in Saint-Rémy. This is where he, amongst other subjects, painted landscapes till his death in 1890.

The Vincent van Gogh Museum owns 230 paintings and 400 drawings by the painter. Next to the Van Gogh Museum you will find the Stedelijk Museum, a museum that specializes in modern art.

The collection at the Stedelijk Museum does not only exists of paintings, but also photographs, functional art, industrial designs and posters.

Highlights are the Malevitsj, Breitner and Chagall collections. The Stedelijk Museum and the Vincent van Gogh Museum are both also very near to the Rijksmuseum which is the largest museum in the Netherlands. The Rijksmuseum dates back to 1885 and was designed by P.J.H. Cuypers.

The 'Nightwatch' is located at the very centre of the building and is admired by more than a million visitors each year.

Since 1952 there are 5 separate departments: Paintings, Sculptures and Applied Arts, Rijks Print Room, Dutch History and Asian Arts.

Naturally the 17th century Dutch painters are well represented. There are 19 works by Rembrandt and paintings by Vermeer, Frans Hals and Jan Steen.

Already during the sixties, the 'Flower Power' time, Amsterdam had a world-wide reputation as a cheerful and tolerant city.

Amsterdam still attracts the most unusual visitors.

Examples of these can be seen around the city. There many meeting places for lesbians and gay boys. The largest international Gay Games, till this date, were held in Amsterdam in 1998. Each year 'Amsterdam Pride' and 'Leather Pride' parades and activities are held in Amsterdam.

Gay-pride through the Herengracht canal

During the Gay Canal Parade a long procession of unusually decorated boats travel along the canals. The enthusiastic people on board are mostly extravertly dressed and they are cheered on from the street by like-minded people. Of course curious citizens and tourists stand along the water to watch the parade go by.

On the Internet you can read a quotation from PR-man Jules Faber: 'Amsterdam is a magical, dynamic, tolerant, greedy, messy, beautiful, enlightened, social feeling, politically active, warm, generous, nice, schizophrenic place'.

Along the Amstel, near the Rembrandtplein there are many gay bars. The 'IT' is the best known gay disco club in the greater Amsterdam area. The hard core gay bars and dancings are located in the middle part of the Warmoesstraat. The target groups from all over the world know about this area.

Singel

Living on an Amsterdam canal is very unique. The 'skippers' have a permanent berth and use a small boat to get around.

The monumental houses along the canals have to abide by all kinds of rules and regulations set by the aesthetic committee and other authorities. The people living on house-boats enjoy the freedom of choosing any exterior they want for their boat.

One boat-owner decides to imitate an Ark of Noah with a complete zoo on it, another just lets the boat be overgrown with plants and bushes to simulate a jungle. Artists living on a boat each have their own way of decorating their home.

Prinsengracht

Sometimes you will see a wreck half in the water. The people that choose to live on house-boats are not just the hippies, recluses, eccentrics or pensioned skippers. Even very fortunate or well educated people, and even a prince, choose this very unique way of housing.

There are approximately 1400 households living on house-boats along the Amsterdam canals. Within the Singelgracht which encloses the old canal system, there are about 750 boats permanently moored.

Nieuwe Keizersgracht

The city council policy is to keep the number of boats within this area fixed and do not issue new mooring licenses any more. The result of this policy is that the prices of the house-boats with a licensed berth have risen enormously. It is practically impossible to even buy a wreck for under 80.000 Dutch guilders.

Herengracht

Almost every boat has electricity, water, telephone and cable television. Under certain circumstances it is even possible to be connected to gas.

It is policy to try and connect every house-boat onto the sewer system before the year 2005.

Flower shops on boats are located along the Singel, between the Munt and Koningsplein, and form a floating flower market. The flowers are displayed on the street.

Herengracht

The richest Amsterdammers had their
'City Palaces' built along the Herengracht, the Keizersgracht and the Prinsengracht. One part of the Herengracht is also known as the 'Golden
Bend'. Romance? Fierce competition?
Tragedy? If the gables could only
speak...

The canal in front of the 'Golden
Bend' along the Herengracht is pur-
posely kept free from house-boats by
the council. Some canals such as the
Brouwersgracht and the northern part
of the Prinsengracht have a high con-
centration of house-boats. House-boat
owners often are troubled by fast
speed boats or other ships that create
waves. Every now and then this can
cause friction.

Elsewhere in this book we mention that the Amsterdam
canal system is flushed every night. Another method of
cleaning the canals is using rafts with water plants growing
on them. These water plants take nutrients out of the water.
These water gardens also offer pleasant nesting facilities for
the many water birds in the city.

Singel

Herengracht

The Bell gable, the Neck gable and the Spout gable stand smartly side by side. The beam in the top holds the lifting block. The bottom part of the house was usually used as storage or as a workplace.

Top: the ships with lea-boards are typically Dutch. The lea-boards enabled flat bottomed ships to sail in shallow water and still maintain course.

In the city centre, a cyclist can cross the distance of 5 kilometres much faster than a car could. Over the last 10 years, the city council has spent 30 million Dutch guilders on cycle paths and tunnels to entice people to use their bicycles more.

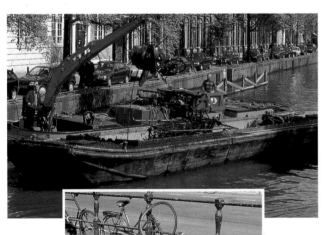

The fact that this plan is not very successful has more to do with how some people use someone else's bicycle. Many bicycles end up in the canal. There are so many bicycles in the water that there is a boat with a special bicycle lifting crane that regularly empties the canals.

There is a story about an Amsterdam glazier that because of bicycle problems missed his boat.

On the day of his office outing on a pleasure boat, the main character in this story was a little late and could not find his bicycle in its usual place. He grabbed the one belonging to his neighbour which, in his haste, got caught between the tram rails. He immediately changed to another 'available' bicycle who's owner chased him down the street, screaming.

Again he jumped off the saddle as an elegant ladies bicycle caught his eye, but did not get very far, after half a kilometre the tyre got a puncture. Funnily enough the reason for the puncture was the sharp point on a Bicycle Union's badge. The aggravated glazier unfortunately found he had missed the boat, but to his amazement found his own bicycle!

Sooner than planned the authorities have recently decided that the bicycle storage areas near stations need to be improved. Expansion of safe parking facilities for bicycles will definitely contribute to the use of public transport.

Singel

Herengracht

Originally Amsterdam had many more canals than it has now. Over twenty of these waterways have been filled in since 1836. Transportation of goods over land slowly expanded. When in 1901 plans were made to fill in the Reguliersgracht, the well-to-do citizens of Amsterdam went to the city hall to protest. This caused a large public discussion which resulted in not filling in any more canals from that date onwards.

Regularly the discussion as to whether the filled in canals should be dug out arises again. The city centre has large traffic problems and when the council actually decides to drastically limit traffic, there could be a possibility of old canals being dug out to bring back transportation over water.

When the ring of canals was constructed the water in it was clean enough to make beer (Brouwersgracht). Unfortunately the people of Amsterdam used the canals as an open sewage.

In early days the city centre smelled very bad during the summer. Rich people that lived along the canals moved away for the summer to their out-of-town house along either the Amstel or the Vecht.

At the end of the 17th century there was an improvement due to a system of sluices that flushed the canal water. The flushings were almost every night. Although the water is not good enough to drink or swim in, the fish are comfortable in it. Anglers can often be seen sitting by the side of the water.

All over Amsterdam you can sit down on nice terraces. Although in danger of generalising we wish to state that in Amsterdam there are 4 areas with places to go out, each with their own character.

At night the Leidse plein and surrounding streets offer the young disco going public places where they can dance and drink till deep into the night. During the day this area is 'dynamic but much quieter'. Tourists gather round the coffee shops, or watch the performing artists.

The Rembrandtplein is more for a mixed and older public. A lot of live music, sung in the Dutch language, can be heard here. The nearby Thorbeckeplein has the usual nightclubs and variety shows. There are a few student cafés here too.

In the Voetboogstraat and the Handboogstraat (better known as 'steeg', meaning alley) is mainly populated by students from the Amsterdam Universities and High Schools. Thursday is the busiest night of the week. When the weather is good there is a large crowd of people outside the cafés. The atmosphere is always very amicable.

The renovated area at the beginning of the Zeedijk and the small streets there are a large number of pubs and places to eat all very close to one another. Tourists, locals and students all come here.

Our advice to you is: do not stay on one terrace for too long, widen your horizon by looking at the lively streets of Amsterdam from different locations. There are also more quiet terraces if that is what you are looking for.

The pubs have contracts with the large breweries. The beers on offer used to be very limited. Nowadays in some pubs you can try a large selection of different kinds and brands of beer. Besides the many old-time pubs with their brown interior, there are now also Grand Cafés. The terraces of these Grand Cafés are usually more spacious, but just as nice. Anyhow, you sit on a terrace to be seen and look around. Though in early spring most people will have their eyes closed and facing the sun.

True Amsterdammers will more often drink in their local pub. This is where their friends come and this is where the local gossip can be heard. If you get talking to the local pub visitor and offer him a beer, you will probably get to hear jokes and tall stories.

Every five years Amsterdam hosts the finish for the Sail Tallship Race. It all started in 1975 when the capital celebrated its 700th year anniversary. The event was very popular with the public and also the crews of the participating ships enjoyed it. The nautical feast attracts at least 1000 ships.

In 1995 over 100 Tall Ships entered, some of them are the largest 'windjammers' in the world. Participants from Russia, Poland, England, France, Norway, Sweden, Italy, Spain and of course the Netherlands took part.

Half of the more than 3.000 crew members were young people aged between 16 and 25. The race started in Edinburgh and finished on the Amsterdam IJ.

One of the highlights of the Sail happening is the 'Sail Parade'. All the ships sail in convoy from Ijmuiden to Amsterdam. Hundreds of pleasure boats and private yachts, all colourfully decorated, accompany them.

On the shores along the route thousands of people watch and later follow on to Amsterdam to take part in the many festivities.

In 1995 'Sail Amsterdam' ended with a fascinating spectacle, mainly organized by the Royal Navy. To close the event there was a spectacular display of fireworks. The pictures on this page are from 1995.

'Sail 2000' (24 august till 28 august 1000) will show the places of call routes. In the right order these will be (April) Southampton - England, Genoa - Italy, (May) Cadiz - Spain, (June) Bermuda, (July) Boston - Massachusetts, and Halifax - Nova Scotia. The parade will be held on 24th august, sailing from Ijmuiden to Amsterdam and will be just as spectacular as previous times.

During the Admiral sailing, the ship greets the Admiral by lowering the foresail and lining the rest of the crew in the gangway.

This ritual dates back to the 12th century and takes about one and a half hour. This 'Admiralty' was originally intended for the defence against attacks from pirates and other enemies.

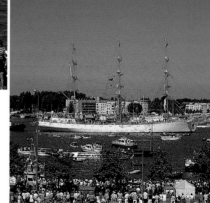

Although the beauty of Amsterdam is extensively described in this book, there are also some less nice issues we need to address.

Any true Amsterdammer will surely tell you two annoying issues: 'parking' and 'dogs fouling the streets'. Lately the problem with dog dirt is improving due to public social behaviour. And the police are more strict about fouling too.

It seems that the parking problems can not be solved by the current city council. The problems have created a centrifugal effect on the city of Amsterdam. Car owners that need to be in the city centre now park their car in areas just outside the centre to avoid fines. This creates a situation whereby the people that live here can hardly find parking spaces which in turn reduces amenity of the area.

Presently the whole area within the ring road A 10 is a paid parking area. This moves the problem to yet another area, Buitenveldert for example. People park there and use public transport into the centre for work or for going home.

In the city centre itself parking garages are being built, often on places where space it 'suddenly' available. Traffic experts say that this is completely incomprehensible.

Traffic experts claim that a solution to the problems should be looked for in building more official Park & Ride areas along the ring road. This can then be combined with good public transport facilities.

'Chain mobility' is the fashionable word for this. The Amsterdam Arena is a good example for a parking solution. But busy business people and unsuspecting tourists will continue to encounter the parking meter and the clamp.

Clamping is a very costly activity for the council and definitely shows a negative side to a city that wishes to be hospitable.

There is a fast tram, number 51, that crosses several motorways (A 9, A 10 and A 12). Unfortunately there no possibilities to leave the car and continue on the tram along the route. According to a spokesperson for the Dutch Automobile Association; if there was a free parking facility and the tram ticket would not be too expensive, it would definitely contribute to making the city centre a nearly car-free zone. The author is of the opinion that travelling by train to Amsterdam is much more pleasant, more comfortable and cheaper than by car. Even if there was enough free Park & Ride parking available.

Many artists are inspired by Amsterdam. Art can literally be found on the streets. Painters have captured the city during the ages with paintings, writers have written about it and songwriters have written songs about Amsterdam. In the tragedy 'De Gysbregt van Aemstel' by Joost van de Vondel performed in night poetry uniquely expresses his feelings. The author gives a historical account of the time during which the construction of the dam and the lock in the Amstel was started to stop the wild waters from the IJ.

Amsterdam has been a great melting-pot of nationalities and religions for hundreds of years. Alternatively it has been a Catholic and a Reformed city. The principle of Freedom of Conscience, which was well founded because of trade interests, has created a three century long tradition of tolerance.

Even outside the country it became clear that in Amsterdam there was a situation where every kind of view and lifestyle were accepted.

Many foreigners, emigrants, artists and intellectuals were drawn to Amsterdam and have contributed to its diversity.

Already in the 17th century the French philosopher Pierre Bayle called Amsterdam 'the great ark for refugees'. This historical character of being a safe haven for the persecuted has continued during the following centuries. At present 25 percent of the population of Amsterdam are immigrants.

The flow of immigration that followed the independence of Suriname in 1975, made Amsterdam the second largest Surinam community in the world. Also many people from the former colony Indonesia came and found a new home in Amsterdam.

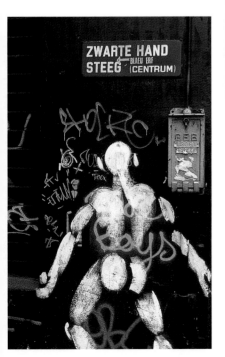

The tolerance can not only be noticed on the streets, but also found in drug and prostitution policies of the city. There is policy to tolerate squatting. At the beginning of the seventies Amsterdam became one of the capitals of squatters movement.

Even the doors in Amsterdam venti-late the philosophy of live and let live. This was already noticeable in the 17th century as the French philosopher Rene Decartes wrote in his letter to a fellow-countryman during his visit to Amsterdam.

   'Where in the world, other than in Amsterdam, can you find the comforts of life and anything that you take pleasure in? Is there any other country where the population have a greater freedom (...).

As any one person knows I lived very contently in my own country and was not forced to move. All frontiers were open to me, any country would gladly have taken me in and yet I chose to live in this country'.

Historically Amsterdam has been a Catholic and Reformed city alternatively. For hundreds of years it has been a melting pot of nationalities and religions. The principle of freedom of conscience is founded on trade interest and has created a three century long strong tradition of tolerance. Even across the borders it became clear that the Amsterdam climate was open to many different opinions and life styles. Many eccentrics, emigrants, artists and intellectuals were drawn to Amsterdam and have contributed to its diversity.

Not only the characteristic and historical canal houses or fine modern architecture of Amsterdam impress the visitor. The playful, original and especially colourful artists and squatters also contribute to the image of the city.

Amsterdam is able to combine the two kinds of exteriors. The postman is less happy as he takes much longer to locate the letter box which in an Amsterdam address can be anywhere at the front of the building.

Flower market on the Amstelveld

Is there any other city in the world that has such a diversity of outdoor and semi-covered markets like Amsterdam? There are 17 markets of which the Albert Cuyp street market is the best known. Stall holders shout out their bargains in broad Amsterdam dialect. Even foreign stall holders carry their voice over the market.

Noordermarkt

Albert Cuyp Market

Besides the daily or weekly markets there are also biological fresh goods markets (Nieuwmarkt and Noordermarkt on Saturday's). The famous art markets are held on Sundays on the Spui and the Thorbecke plein.

The Nieuwmarkt also holds a market with antiques, art, book and bric-á-brac on Sundays.

Gassan Diamonds

In 1586 the diamond-cutter Willem Vermaet moved from Antwerp to Amsterdam. This Huguenot can be considered to be the founder of the diamond industry in Amsterdam. His work was continued by the Portuguese jews. During the 17th century they made Amsterdam into the European Centre of Diamond cutting and diamond trade.

The 'Cullinan' and the 'Koh-I-Noor' which is the largest diamond found in the world, are some of best known diamonds that were cut in Amsterdam.

But also the smallest diamond, 0.00012 carat was cut with 57 facets here.

The three main tasks for normal shaped stones are sawing, cutting and more cutting. Irregular diamonds can be split.

Nowadays mining for diamonds and cutting diamonds both use a lot of electronic equipment.

(You will find more details on page 2)

A large number of tourists would like
to take a look at a diamond workshop.
This is possible. There are several dia-
mond-cutting establishments that
have well organized tours. It is also
possible to purchase a mysterious
'sparkler' set in either a brooch, a ring
or pendant for a reasonable price.

"Gassan Diamonds"

Noord-Zuid Hollands Koffiehuis

Even in winter visitors to Amsterdam do not have to miss the view of the sights from the water. The sight-seeing boats will remain moored as seen here at the Noord-Zuid Hollands Coffee House.

When the canals are frozen over visitors as well as the Amsterdam population will walk on the ice and enjoy the unique view of the city. When the water is frozen over, which does not happen every winter, there will definitely be traditionally Dutch ice-scating on the canals.

A wintry tour along the canals is clearly pleasant and rustic which is in contrast to the colourful and lively summer months.

Keizersgracht

Especially in winter, dressed in white, the elegant top of the Montelbaans Tower seems to show the imperishable character that monuments have. They can be considered as beacons of time, marked by their time but still standing.

Montelbaanstoren

Near the Zandhoek (Sand corner) on the Reaal Island is where the sand used for ballast on ships was stored. Here the row of thirty gables, each with their own character, form an authentic front on the Westerdok (quay).

In the days long gone by it used to be a bustling place of activity which only a cold winter could bring to a halt.

Zandhoek

Everyone knows that the modern Coffee shops have nothing to do with the coffee and tea houses that used to be in the capital. Soft drugs such as hash and marihuana are mainly sold here.
Only small amounts are sold here, but still...

Opponents of these drugs should look back at the time of prohibition in America. Crime rates rose tremendously. Trade in hard drugs is not tolerated by the Dutch authorities.

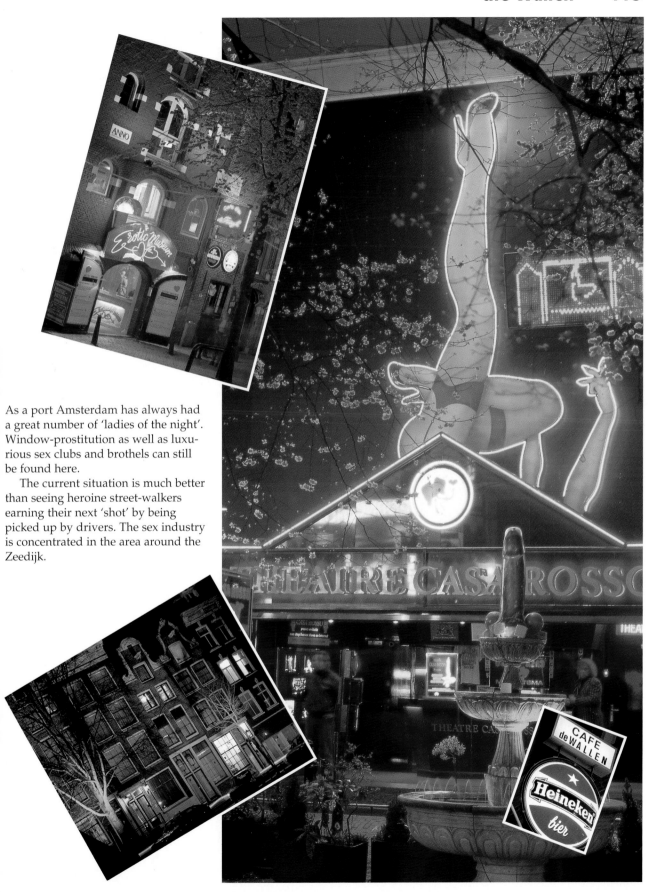

As a port Amsterdam has always had a great number of 'ladies of the night'. Window-prostitution as well as luxurious sex clubs and brothels can still be found here.

The current situation is much better than seeing heroine street-walkers earning their next 'shot' by being picked up by drivers. The sex industry is concentrated in the area around the Zeedijk.

Even at night Amsterdam still retains its historic beauty. Due to the carefully chosen lighting the unique collection of gables can be seen in a different light. The canals can be recognized indirectly by the shining of the magical lights of the bridges on the water.

Damrak

Many artists have been inspired by Amsterdam. The city has been immortalized by paintings since a long time. Artist have been driven to write or sing about Amsterdam. Also nightly poetry is very well delivered here. An example of this is the tragedy 'De Gysbregt van Aemstel' by Joost van den Vondel.

Skinny Bridge

With this tragedy he was able to paint a historical picture of the time when the dam was being built and when lock in the river Amstel held back the wild water of the IJ.

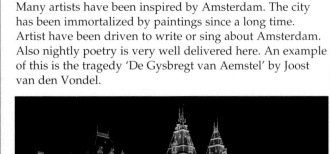

Rijksmuseum

In the darkness of the night Amsterdam displays her most beautiful sights. Floodlit orientation points such as the Montelbaans Tower give comfort, while other aspects of the city's mysterious atmosphere are lit up.

The replica of the East-Indies ship 'Amsterdam' looks melted in timelessness of darkness and water. For a moment it seems like it is 1749 and she has just returned from a trip to the East. (The original ship went down before the coast of Hastings, England in 1749).

The Maritime Museum building which used to be where the goods were stored for the Verenigd Oostindische Companie (United East Indies Company) is floodlit to create, together with the 'Amsterdam', a scenery for the time that the merchant fleet sailed the seas.

In 1602 the many trading-companies that traded with Southwest Asia united under the V.O.C. flag. The V.O.C. set up a number of factories in the East Indies, Ceylon and Tasmania.

To strengthen their monopoly it concentrated on East Asia and even Japan for the import of tea, sugar, silk, enamel and porcelain. Following competition from the English and French the V.O.C. lost ground and finally disappeared from the scene completely at the end of the 18th century.

Montelbaans Tower   *Maritime Museum*

New Metropolis, designed by Renzo Piane, looks futuristic during the day so when floodlit at night the 'science and technology centre' looks even more so. It is built above the entrance to the IJ tunnel. The walls are covered with oxidated copper which at night is more visible. This material is not only easy to maintain, it also is a perfect example to combining technology and science in architecture.

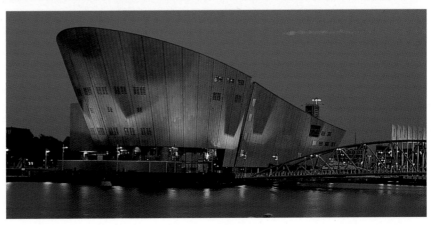

New Metropolis

Amsterdam by night clearly speaks to the imagination. A fine example of this is the Dam.

There you can see the Royal Palace nicely lit and it brings back the memories of the good times when receptions, parties or inaugurations were held here.

Such an event was in 1948. It was when Queen Wilhelmina emotionally introduced her daughter Juliana as the new Queen of the Netherlands to the people. The two women stood on the balcony that dated back to Louis Napoleon.

At the front of the Palace there is a 10 metre wide strip of small stones, which used to be where only the sentries were allowed to walk.

The reason for this is the story of a sentry that found a baby that had been abandoned in his sentry-box. Queen Hortense, wife of Louis Napoleon, felt sorry for the infant and granted it an annual allowance. To prevent this happening again the area with the 'small stones' became out of bounds for the public.

This ban was not lifted until the 1920's when the sentries were abolished.

You can definitely feel and recognize the history of this city in its monuments. Despite everything Amsterdam remains a unique city with a charming mixture of grand manners and vulnerability.

During whatever season you visited the city, the character of the old city centre the same. The varied views and the logical chaos can be recognized as the city of Amsterdam. We have a monumental capital that is still in touch with the human side of life.

It is such a unique place that photographs describe her best. During the evening you can look into the water where the Singel and the Amstel come together, the Muntplein and experience a sense of depth in what you see.

The Munt Tower ('coin tower) is on this spot. It is the rectangular tower which used to be a part of the Regulierspoort (gate) built in 1490. When the gate burned down in 1619, only the bottom part survived.

Munt Tower

The municipality commissioned Hendrick de Keyser to design a wooden top for the stone base. The name of the Munt Tower comes from the fact that money was coined here.

Herengracht

To begin with the Herengracht was a narrow moat and was not widened to its current width until the extension in 1613. Along the Herengracht there are still 61 double houses. These beautiful houses nearly all stand next to one another along the part of the canal located between the Leidsegracht and the Reguliersgracht: the Golden Bend.

'Amsterdam ArenA'

Not only in the city centre, but also in the South-East district of Amsterdam you can see a spectacular sea of lights at night. As soon as it is dark the World Trade Center, the Academic Medical Center, the Arena and the blocks of offices and shopping malls offer a magical spectacle of light.

This gigantic stadium is the home to probably Holland's best known football club 'Ajax'. It can be reached very easily from the Amsterdam ring road. Dedicated fans will definitely want to visit the Ajax museum and merchandising shop. There are regular tours around the building.

The stadium is famous for its sliding roof and infamous for the turf. The turf has needed to be replaced regularly. The so-called Transferium is very important at the Arena. It offers extensive parking facilities to visitors to the match or other large events held in the Arena. These facilities can also be used by people who want to travel into the city centre. Visitors to the nearby World Trade Center park here too.

The Amsterdam Arena is now also famous for the many different large events that are held here. Two examples of these are pop concerts and a complete winter sport facility.

The office and business park called Amsterdam-Zuidoost (South-East Amsterdam) is located between the capital and Schiphol (Amsterdam Airport). This is where fantastic modern architecture and international activity come together.

This area is much better accessible from the ring road and by public transport than the old city centre.

There are two active World Trade Centers. On the picture you can see the one located along the ring road, near the RAI complex. The second WTC is on the Schiphol Boulevard.

Rembrandt Tower

South-East Amsterdam

During the Golden Age the traffic on the IJ was very busy. Nowadays it is much less busy. The port of Rotterdam has become more important. Any port activity has been moved more west.

Not far from Amsterdam Central Station is the cruise ships terminal for ships such as the 'Maasdam'. Over half a million passengers travel by ship to a foreign harbour. The number of cruise ships that visit Amsterdam is increasing so much that a new terminal has been planned.

At the end of the 19th century a canal was dug to create a shorter connection between Amsterdam and the North Sea (North Sea Canal). Amsterdam then became a port with scheduled sailings organized by shipping companies located at the port.

Slowly the tendency of the port changed towards stowage and people tried to gain new business in transport of goods. Due to this the harbour was expanded extensively at the end of the 1960's. The eastern part of the harbour area used to be dominated by Maatschappij Nederland (Dutch Indies), Royal Holland Lloyd (South America) and the KNSM (Mediterranean, USA and the 'West').

Presently this area is visited by Japanese ships that deliver their load to the different car giants. Following the opening of the North Sea Canal the industry in North Amsterdam developed itself due to the economic prosperity. Refineries and shipyards were set up here.

Despite the recession during the 1980's there was a considerable growth in the trans-shipment of goods in the Amsterdam harbour. The increase came from the mass trans-shipping of North Sea oil.

Generally container shipments are more profitable than individual goods shipments, even in the traditionally Amsterdam cocoa business. Indonesian shipping companies still visit the harbour. Around 20 percent of the world's cocoa bean harvest is transported to Amsterdam harbour.